BOX

BOX

ROBERT WRIGLEY

PENGUIN POETS

PENGUIN BOOKS

An imprint of Penguin Random House LLC
375 Hudson Street
New York, New York 10014
penguin.com

Pages 67–68 constitute an extension of this copyright page.

LIBRARY OF CONGRESS CATALOGING-IN-PUBLICATION DATA
Names: Wrigley, Robert, 1951– author.
Title: Box / Robert Wrigley.
Description: New York : Penguin Books, [2017] | Series: Penguin Poets
Identifiers: LCCN 2016047476 (print) | LCCN 2016058325 (ebook) |
ISBN 9780143130567 (softcover) | ISBN 9781524704131 (ebook)
Subjects: | BISAC: POETRY / American / General.
Classification: LCC PS3573.R58 A6 2017 (print) | LCC PS3573.R58 (ebook) |
DDC 811/.54—dc23
LC record available at https://lccn.loc.gov/2016047476

Printed in the United States of America
1   3   5   7   9   10   8   6   4   2

Set in New Caledonia
Designed by Ginger Legato

for Kim

for my mother, Betty

and in memory of my father,
Arvil William Wrigley (1922–2014)

CONTENTS

Its life-span is shorter even than that of the perishables it encloses.

—Francis Ponge

But salvation here? What about the rattle of sticks
On tins and boxes? What about horses eaten by wind?

—Wallace Stevens

MY PEOPLE

Not having any money never made them
think badly of the moon's monthly vanishing.
Besides, there was scientific expertise to be gleaned
from beans and a slingshot squab. Also gravy.
Their driveways were paved with coal-stove clinkers.
An outhouse forgave all sins without confession.

Any star that shone in the morning was a blessing
upon them. The problem with newspapers
was that they were owned. Coal dust seeded
their lungs with the nights they would not live to see.
Train whistles moaned, kindly and beneficent.
Elsewhere was another myth they did not believe.

Bent as he became, my grandfather found a thousand
quarters and purchased a thousand beers therewith.
He was thirty when he married my grandmother,
who was not quite sixteen and loved his graceful way
on the dance floor. My father almost finished fifth grade
and half a century later built a grandfather clock.

Rumor always had it there was a picture somewhere
of the person they called "Old Man Wrigley,"
gum magnate and millionaire. He sat right there with them,
in the old unplumbed, foundationless, immaculate house.
No one ever found the picture but they still believed
the old man the relative he was claimed to have been.

Socialists and anarchists, mostly, they disapproved
of Democrats but despised Republicans.
The few who became cops were forgiven. Several died
in wars. Their graves are scattered all over

Bluff Hill Cemetery, sometimes a husband and wife
with a stranger, or even two, between them.

They would not know what to make of this work
I do, which would not seem to them like work at all.
Three years ago, I rolled my father's wheelchair
to the grave of his namesake, Great-Uncle Arvil.
Ninety-two, with Parkinson's, my father didn't say much
but said, as he always said, "Shit, I hate that name."

.

ECOLOGY

Study the muddy house, the salmon
gutting it out through glacial till.
Study the heart, which should not be seen
but heard. Study the tree that is the child

and the ink that makes an octopus invisible.
Epistemologies of silence and blindness,
suffering of common stones, the soul
with its hardened, scaly, inevitable callus:

study them by coyote light, buffalo magnification.
Study the imperatives of rain and snow
at the whim and fancy of the wind.
Study wind as well. We will never know

what it desires beyond the elsewhere it is going.
Study elsewhere, the geography of strange beds
and topographies of lips, the glowing,
enormous, indefatigable possibilities of red.

The sky, which is the mother of all rivers,
must be studied, as must the river of all mothers,
those oceans of spirit, the wells of unbelievers,
days like buckets full, arriving one after another

in the absence of an invisible engineer.
Study the balusters and balustrades, wall studs
of sedimentary stone, the skin, the downiest hair.
Study spring grass, the planetary grave, the blood-fed

soil of the body farm, the pentagrammatic arm.
Study the cuticle and free margin parentheses enclosing

pink implications, the vast concupiscent charms
of the toes, the sleepy eye's slow closing.

In such time as you are given, study the house
within the house within the house you love in.
Know of it such portion as you are allowed,
and return to it to die, like a salmon.

BLESSED ARE

you, faithful ravens, for staying on and saying
through the songbirdless winter
the Biblical syntax of your declarations.

It is with interest I watch you excise,
with inordinate patience, the upward eye
of the fallen deer below the house,

and the sight through my binoculars
puts me eye-to-eye with you
and the eye you eat and squabble over,

opening now and then your wings
in excitable Corvidae vexations,
like a scrum of omnivorous umbrellas.

Further plunder will require your partners, the coyotes,
slinking even now your way, awaiting
the night your plumage exemplifies

and under which they will open the carcass
for your further delectation and caws—
a dozen mornings I imagine it will take.

Then the snows will bury it, and many mice
will gnaw its bones, until it emerges yet again
from the melts of spring, a blessing for the blowflies

and the seethe of their maggots, until the vault
the empty brain occupied is emptied itself,
and I retrieve the skull and hang it on my shack.

There it will be filled with thoughts of yellow jackets.
There it will grin its grim, unmandibled
half smile out over the distances swallows

troll for the yellow jackets themselves,
and one of you will perch upon a bare rib then,
to recite, for all the world, your ravenous beatitudes.

TINNITUS

—at the library

The loneliness of a rank of six public
pay phones moves me today almost to tears,
and I wonder, dropping in my quarters,
if you will allow this odd nostalgic

impulse toward anachronism
to go through. That is, if you will answer
this morning's call from an unknown number,
or let it, by the cold mechanism

of that which is called caller ID,
be rerouted to what is known as voice mail.
And then, on hearing your unreal voice, if I will,
nevertheless, tell you that it's me.

But no, I hang up, and from the pay phone
on the far right I call the one one slot left,
and from the third, call the next one left,
and from the fifth, call the sixth and final phone,

creating as I do a carillon
of overlapping, almost identical rings,
disturbing the many students studying
in this building, where no one's home.

As I leave, I dial you on my cell phone,
and you answer, asking if I've just called,
saying the number was strange, that you'd called
back but heard only a busy-signal's drone.

Ah, love, let us be true to one another
in almost every way, I also do not say.

I'm at the door now, this cold and snowy day,
thinking of the old high ways one lover

once spoke to another, over wires,
when a call could be a complete surprise.
Still you ask, what is that strange bell noise?
And I answer, just the ringing in my ears.

THEE

You should know I would rather say thou shouldst
to you. Or speaking objectively, thee.
And you should know, if I wanted to, I couldst,
but won't—no, wait, yes I will, intermittently.

Thy face, thine eyes—my first example, this.
What these lose with "your" seems little enough,
not much more than kiss't instead of kissed.
Some think this just so much poetic fluff,

but I love the implication of the apostrophe—
that what's left out's a sort of fine indecency.
And how better than dull -ed the touch of that t,
given what I know of your lips, and of thee.

Thy lips, I should have said. It's more emphatic,
insist the linguists, regarding the one addressed,
who is thee and why I like it, this dusty archaic
lingo, as in, without thy clothes, thou art undressed.

Thine for that of yours beginning with a vowel,
and thy for every consonantal part. Of thee, I mean.
Or you. And A, E, I, and O, of course, the other vowels:
Thine instep, thy pate, thy fingertips, and what's between,

or betweenest, of thee. The nominative is thou,
the objective thee; i.e., thou art thee,
and my objective, and this must end soon now,
if I am fortunate, and thou shalt soon be thee with me.

A FINE BOY

Above all, this one memory, otherwise insignificant:
the front passenger seat of a new 1957 Volkswagen Beetle,
my feet almost touching the floor, the radio on—big band tunes
from St. Louis—and my father, having shifted to third,
extends his hand farther right and places it on my knee,
which he pats three times. Then he tells me, "You're a fine boy."

It was the sort of thing he would have said.
I don't remember ever hearing it before or after that day,
but I recall the rush of ecstasy that came with it,
and I remember how he smiled saying it,
so that it was something I could believe, although
I had no idea, not one, regarding what it might mean.

We did not know one another very well in those days.
He had two jobs. He was always working, even on Sunday—
which this must have been—doing all the things around the house
he had no other time to do. Except on this particular Sunday
we were going somewhere together. I can't remember where,
or why, but now I was a fine boy and I believed I was.

There isn't anything else to it, really. No arrival, no departure.
Not even the journey itself. I don't remember
if we crossed the river or if he said anything else along the way.
I was six. What else does one say to a six-year-old?
"You're a fine boy," he said, and that was enough.
And now, fifty-eight years after the fact, it's all there is.

Three or four thrilling seconds of my life to that point, or more.
I'm sure I said nothing in return. I hardly spoke to him then.
I would not have known what to say. The car, as his cars always were,
was impossibly clean—gleaming even. I would not have touched

a thing, not the window crank—I think it must have been summer—
or the dash. My hands would have stayed in my lap the whole way.

And the way might have been nowhere. It might have been
no more than a ride. He liked to go for rides in his cars. He liked
to admire the reflection of his car in the windows of the stores
we passed on Main Street. He liked big band music and so did I.
Eventually, I would begin to disappoint him, but I did not know it then.
It was not an imaginable thing, disappointing him, nor imaginable how.

He was a strange and loving man, with a bad temper now and then,
and strangest of all, long, sculpted, even womanly fingernails, so long
my aunts, who adored him, would sometimes speak of them in envy.
He might have tapped them on the VW's horn button as he drove—
later I would see him do that, in other cars, and wonder about it.
I didn't know who he was, and I wasn't anyone, just a fine boy,

whatever that meant. I was scrawny, but not as scrawny as he had been
at the age I was. As for baseball, he did not understand it, or any other sport.
He did not understand the point of games. He understood work
and the internal combustion engine, but he did not understand me,
nor I him. That would take years. I understood his strangeness
before I knew what it was. I still do not know exactly what it was.

And I still do not know exactly who I am, and I am sixty-four,
and he has been dead just over six months. He could fix anything.
Anything that broke he fixed, making it better than it had been.
With the possible exception of me, although it was I who'd break myself,
in a way that defied hand tools, in a way that defied even hands,
even his on my knee that day. It was invisible, except when it wasn't.

The temper, maybe. Which for him produced brief and intense strings
of obscenities, usually directed at things, but sometimes, later, at me,
who would respond in kind, and who would come to know such things

as those broken that way are broken sometimes beyond repair.
I couldn't have known that then. I didn't know it for a long time, for years.
But on that day, just that once that I recall, I was a fine boy.

There was big band music on the radio. Probably there was sunshine.
I was sitting up front, where I hardly ever sat. I could almost see
out the windshield. He tapped his long fingernails on the horn button,
or he didn't. Given the enormous significance of his touch,
I think I must have been wearing short pants. The skin of his hand
against the skin of my knee, three times, four words. That's all I remember.

BECAUSE THE MOUNTAIN DWARFS THE GROVE, THE SKY THE MOUNTAIN

Some botanists have proffered a theory
that a stand of aspens—what we call a grove—
is in fact a single organism, and that therefore
the largest living thing on the planet must be
just such a stand of trees, much like the grove

I am at this very moment lying in or on
or among the many-ringed arboreal embodiments of,
each of which, because it is late October,
is ablaze inside its typical quaking, in the annual
gold of its slow descent into dormancy,

and many of the limbs are now letting such gold go,
so that reclined as I am upon it or among them,
I am within no more than a few minutes myself
made golden, blanketed by their or its spadelike leaves
even as a million more quiver elegantly above me,

as though, though I know otherwise, it or they approve
of my presence and consent to cover me
as must be my wish, since I do not rise
but, rather, blow away the occasional one fallen on my eyes,
so that I might see each delicate hand of them

or it above me, although the leaves will not all fall
this afternoon, and already the autumn cold
has worked its way through my jacket and into my limbs
and bones, as I peer upward into the last light
of the setting sun and shiver, just as they do.

HIS PREVIOUS LIFE AS A LICHEN

He did not go far, and the journey was long.
      It seemed his quest was to enact the shadow
of a distant ridge, until it was the distant ridge

that became somehow the shadow of him.
      This freed him to swaddle an entire stone,
to be a cloak, to gown the gray granite of a cog

in a mountain's machinery, to be the skin of it,
      to feed it such moisture as he could sift
from rain and snow and wind. He was happy.

Everything he thought became him.
      Everything was the same. He knew his place
and his place was everywhere he could feel.

The fire that killed him released his spirit,
      and a woman breathed it and became
his grandmother, who planted a moss garden

behind her house. At first he did not know why
      he loved the place so much. Then the wild lichen
that had attached itself to the ear of a stone rabbit

spoke to him in a tongue he understood, a calling.
      Speak of the silence. Say nothing not a secret
to the world. Kiss the earth for all your life.

FROM THE PERSPECTIVE OF THE MEADOW

It did not begin with the sight of the airplane—
a contrail first, then a flash
at the head of it, the fuselage in the sun.
He was lying on his back in a meadow
of long grasses, listening
to a gang of elk graze around him:
hoof thumps, rips of torn blades,
grinds of mastication. From the trees
around the meadow edges the songs
of birds he could not identify.
Shadows of grass swayed
across his face. The sun a kiss,
the shadows caresses. The elk, being upwind,
would startle when one of them came
upon him and run for the trees.
But then he saw the contrail of the jet
and an ant walking near the very tip
of a stalk of grass, then the flash
from the fuselage, half the size of
and moving hardly as fast as the ant,
which made him smile.
And there he was, half-asleep, smiling,
at just the moment a cow elk
poked her head into what he had almost come
to believe was his personal space,
as grand a bedroom as any prince's,
where he lay attended to by long bluestem,
or maybe it was buffalo grass, his bed
a hundred acres large, where he was surprised
by a goddess grazing, and where a tiny black
dragon strode a tall green leaf, reaching for,
but failing to capture, an angel.

OR POSSIBLY LANGUOR

So many words for it lovelier than
what they describe: lassitude, torpor,

lethargy, ennui. Phalanges of lead,
the lifting of eyelids requiring hydraulic force.

I am interested in the fact that lassitude—
the word, that is—has declined

in use by nearly fifty percent
over the last two centuries; lethargy

likewise, by almost as much. Also
that enervation peaked around 1875,

along with ennui. How can that be?
And torpor, if linguists and lexicographers

are correct, is almost all gone now.
Indolence thrives, however, even though

or perhaps because it is November,
even the local birds afflicted with it.

This rumpled nuthatch, for instance,
having sidled along the deer rib perch

from the nubbined spinal end
to the very point at which the bone's screwed

to the porch post, where the bird sprawls
against the cedar and does not sing at all.

RAVEN IN APRIL
reading Plath and Hughes

This morning I was her, regarding red poppies
from the window. Then I was him, ventriloquizing
the black bird of God. Her, bewildered; and him,
another sanctified animal he ought to have been
and unhappy he was not. As I was, being him
or his bird and not her. Then, because it is spring
and not October, and the bird outside my window
a raven, its black left eye peering in at me
with the enormous and caustic curiosity of its kind,
I was neither her nor him, but myself,
and I studied the dark bolts of its talons clamped
on the broken stob that is the gnomon
of the afternoon's sundial, its shadow
by the minute rising up the western window.
Black ravages, negative lightning, sleek oily sheen,
and my god, the bottomless eye, wondering what it is
there is to say, about what I am.

STILLNESS, WAITING

If the trout died it would not be
as motionless as it is now,
in a current a man cannot
stand in and under which looser
stones go tumbling from their sockets.
Across its back it seems sunlight
is what's swimming, and still the trout
is still, not the least fin flick or
tail motion, but a curve of meat
held in the river's swift rushing.

Only then the Skwala stonefly
drifts above it and, unbending,
the trout rises, drifting upward,
and slurps the fly from the surface,
then sinks back down to where it was,
resuming its stillness, too deep
for even the spring's last eagles,
and believing, if it sees me
at all, that I must be no more
than a tree or a tree's shadow.

I move, like all shadows, slowly,
almost imperceptibly, east,
on such an afternoon as this,
when the river has lost its ice
and the first fat terrestrials
have hatched, so that fish might again
feed, after the long dark winter.
And this is how it is I am—
moving more slowly than I can—
in perfect position to cast

my feathery simulacrum
of the sort of bug just eaten,
that it might drift on the current
exactly as the real thing had
moments or even years ago,
when, infinitesimally,
I made my way to where I am,
and concentrated, and did not
give myself away, but waited,
just as I am waiting right now.

For the fierceness of the long fight,
run and reclaim, leap and tail-walk,
patience and deep concentration;
the netting and admiration,
gratitude, and the quick release;
a gentle holding of the trout
in the wash of a hard current,
as it recovers and bolts off.
Forgive me, we are not there yet.
Even now, my fly in its drift

has not yet entered the trout's ken.
It is moving as shadows move.
Its motion is planetary.
This day's same sun will set and rise
a million times or more before
what is is permitted to be.
The river glideth, you might say,
at his own sweet will, as does time,
which I am in charge of just now,
as otherwise I never am.

MIO DIO
the first morning

Slowly rising out of sleep, I am hauled up
on a line of sound from a dream already
forgotten: it was a woman's voice,
a woman neither saying nor singing but being lifted—
as I am being lifted out of sleep—
by what it is she does not say or sing
but expresses more clearly than words
or melody can: she is bound for a destination.
Now I am too. Except it turns out where
is only morning, although it is morning
in Assisi, a blessing all by itself.
As for the woman who lifted me up,
she's just a pigeon, though one possessed of the most
melodious and aubadial voice I have ever heard.
She is calling it on and calling me with it—
a day like any other, if you are a pigeon,
or a woman, or even a man, and the line of the sun
has only begun to begin where you are,
but you can almost taste it coming.

JASMINE

Once I thought—in truth, I still do—
that music might have been
the art I was better suited to.
Knowing this and still thinking so
is another issue altogether. It dawns on me
this afternoon in Italy, thousands of miles
from my dictionaries and without
a decent Internet connection, that *talent*
is a word I do not think I can define,
let alone offer its derivation.
The owner of this lovely rental house
in Assisi did not lie about the Internet
connection but e-mailed, in a broken
English more functional than my Italian,
"an internet is in the house." But you should see
how he's bound with simple kitchen twist ties
a piece of eight-millimeter rebar
to two iron brackets protruding
from the front of his house, and along which now
great white clouds of jasmine burst.
Their sweet scent is what I breathe for hours today.
But it's not the jasmine I mean for you to see.
It's the rebar: common steel but unlike the American version
not just ribbed with nubbins each quarter inch, but swirled
in an elegant spiral from one end to the other.
Even the rebar usually entombed in concrete
is beautiful here. Once, I used to be able to sing
anything. The choir director in junior high exclaimed,
"You've got a four-and-a-half-octave range!"
and gave me that aggrieved-teacher look
when I quit chorus and bought a guitar and learned

a thousand chords and how they fit together
but fell eventually upon this. I mean the way the rebar
holds the jasmine, the way the blossoms
ask for all the attention and never say a word
and are the stage for the million arias of the bees.

S. FRANCESCO

Lording it over the others, the ones
perched not upon the chimney top
but arrayed as vassals around
and below him, this pigeon potentate
in the midst of his preening and posturing
is seized by a kestrel or a small hawk
of a genus I do not recognize—
the Italian version of a sharp-shinned,
maybe: it appeared in its high-
speed swoop an instant before its talons
took hold of the pigeon's neck
and shoulders. A thin bleat,
a poof of feathers and dust—
then gone, soaring down the north slope
of Monte Subasio, probably to alight
on the branches of an olive tree,
one of the thousands visible from here,
just east of and slightly higher than
the famous basilica of Saint Francis,
who without reservation also loved them both.

SHEEP IN UMBRIA

Now the sheep have gathered together again.
They look like a pile of golden stones
from this distance. They are Appenninica sheep.

This last statement may not be true, even though
Appenninica are common throughout Umbria
and Tuscany, and even to the east, in the Marche.

Mostly, I just love to write and read the word
Appenninica. Appenninica, Appenninica.
The Appenninica sheep are resting or asleep

in a pasture of olive trees. O, rest easy, America.
I am keeping my keen eye on the Appenninica.

BROTHER TO JACKDAWS

I want wings. I want to look
like every other jackdaw—
mostly black, my nape, neck,
and cheeks a modest gray.

I want to catch this wind
coming in from the east,
a spice of Adriatica in it.
I want to soar to the west

halfway to Perugia then return.
I want to perch right over there,
on one of those lichen-burnished
roof tiles, and let the air

have its way with my plumage.
I want to keep my eye
on the man who leaves coinage
on his windowsill. Why?

That is something I would know.
And also everything
about being a Eurasian jackdaw,
and finally nothing

about being a man: not why
I would leave a coin on a sill,
but why for me? Why would I,
a jackdaw, feel compelled,

as I do now, this third day
in a row, to take what he presents?
I want to perch across the way
from him, on that perfect roof vent,

and wait, then making my move
glide over to his sill, his meaty claws
only inches from me, and seize
the coin—bravest of the jackdaws!—

then carry it to my nest
and leave it among the others
that, in his generosity, he has left,
my dark-eyed flightless brother.

I thought he might be dead the first time.
He was asleep on a stone bench, in a nook
high on the via S. Croce. The night before
had been cool. He lay on his left side
on the worldwide standard scavenged
slab of cardboard. No sign of breathing,
but then I saw beneath the eyelids a movement
in him, inside his dreaming mind.

The second time I was wandering
among the tiny and mostly unnamed *vicoli*
in the vicinity of Chiesa Nuova, noting
hundreds of potted flowers on the walls,
the curiosities of millennium-old architecture,
and there he was, beneath a stairway.
Only this time my walking awakened him,
his head snapping up in belligerence and fear.

The third and final time was just outside
the Porta Perlici, on my way up to Rocca
Maggiore, that citadel once the home of dukes
and kings. He was awake this time,
and uttered a single-word question: "Sigaretta?"
I had a pack with three inside and gave them all
to him, with a lighter. I wanted to ask him
things and might have, with more Italian.

I could have asked, "How are you?" or
"What's your name?" Or even, "Senza casa?"
which I thought was something close to
"Are you homeless?" But how *stupido* did I wish
to appear? What I would have liked to ask

was why wouldn't the city of Saint Francis be
the best place in the world for one in your situation?
Or better yet, what happened to you?

Why are you here? That is, why are you
senza casa in the city of Saint Francis?
Instead, I gave him the coins in my pocket—
three or four euros. That was two weeks ago.
No sign of him since. How does anyone in Assisi
not see Saint Francis in a homeless man?
It's true, he wasn't preaching to the birds
or convincing the swallows to quiet down

so that he might. He wasn't taming a wolf.
If there's a wolf in these domesticated mountains
anywhere, I would expect to find Francis with it.
The man sucked so hard on the first cigarette
he consumed half of it in a single drag.
The day after I saw him that final time,
we went to the basilica to visit Francis's tomb again,
which is stately and simple, as fitting,

but which, from the Giotto frescoes to the gold
reliquaries in the museum, is surrounded
by things of enormous economic value,
all of which is owned by the church, and all of which—
you know absolutely this is true—
someone, given the opportunity, would buy,
and someone else would sell, taking the proceeds
to do the kinds of things you dream of with money.

MOTHER COUNTRY

1. Besides the People
   ". . . there is his knowledge of himself." —Stevens

There is the fascination of a herd of elk.
About a herd of elk, which is fascinating,
there is the fascination of the elk
about the world, most especially the people,
of which, in this case, there is only one.

In the enormous eyes of the elk
a man sees the fascination he inspires,
which is particular, a secret longing
to understand both
hooflessness and lack of horns.

Precisely the mystery he too, in the midst
of a late autumn morning in the mountains,
would confront and parse.
He parts the tall grasses walking.
The elk also part the grasses walking.

There is mist in the air analogous
to nothing. There is frost
turning the seed heads and blades to minarets.
His hands, open palmed and thumbed
to his temples, are his horns.

Everywhere the trampled spots
where the elk have bedded down
and risen from, the herd opening for him
so that he is almost elk himself where he is.
He has no secrets from them.

The cows are quickened, the bulls
have put away their drive.
The winter is long and will kill one
in four and still their fascination
keeps them all where they are.

The bulls' horns stir the mist, the cows
around the man bark in the way
of cows. The bulls neither bugle
nor prance. The man's hands flex once
and the last elk still grazing looks up stunned.

If you were this man, would you sing now?
If you would, would you sing
of the scent of them, which is wild, a tincture
of stale musk, a counterpoint of fear?
Would the mist of your song join the mist in the air,

which is nothing? No matter. The thunder as they run
drums the land and the man understands
they understand his hands are hands, not horns,
and he stands, the knot at the heart of the paths
through the meadow grasses' blasted frost.

There is a world inside this world.
There is a knot, a wayward knot, not to be
undone by anyone. When they run,
the man is alone in the meadow.
The elk are dust of what he is not.

2. Paradise Trailer Park
    ". . . in paradise, / Itself non-physical . . ." —Stevens

Many are the places christened by men so called,
and many are the men who would make it so,

if making were only will and hand,
ledger lines and force. Of course heaven
must have snowy mountains and saguaro,
vineyards and vivid women, not the least rumor
of televised executions nor legislative merriment,
but a blue sea, great storms, and students of the clouds.

The deer leaping back and forth across a fence
expresses a joy the bones and desiccated hide
of its fellow tangled in the strands
cannot resummon, but what is paradise
if it features no bones, no sexual innuendos
of requisite blossoms, no magisterial needs
a student of the clouds should perceive?
Heaven's perception is conceived in the flesh.

In the absence of dancing, there is violence.
The dump of empire, the backwash of Zion,
Nirvana of need, absolution in unsatisfactory ways.
The ways of the men inventing paradise
havoc cactus, perfect vineyards pillaged by birds.
This impoverished trailer park,
under its sagging sign, is someone's heaven,
the only child here, a boy who loves to dance.

3. January Chinook
     "Lakes are more reasonable than oceans." —*Stevens*

All day the snow fell, a foot of it
accumulated, and in the night the snow
disengaged from its geometrical designs,
becoming the most ordinary of cold rains,
and he is, in the morning, very sad.
The sodden chapeau on the weathervane,
once a mimic of the pyramidal pines,

has slumped to a watery oozing beret,
and about that he is bereft.

Still, into the deliquescing world he goes,
considering liquefaction, sentiment,
and slush, the mush his footsteps gray,
the way the just-add-water earth
dispenses scents worthy of contemplation.
Fungal things, cold meat, the *tout de suite*
too sweet life rush gushed up from death,
and he thinks, *How can it be that God,*
which is everything, has no mother?

And imagining everything's mother,
he imagines a God whose skin the snow was,
whose skin the meat and fungal bouquet
must be, a planetary pelvis from which
continually blossoming comes the rain.
Brew of imbroglio entered on foot,
slush slick, mud slick, a broth
of dereliction and continuity, the fact
that sadness is the fine thrum of time.

Everywhere the *rat-a-tat* of melts
and rivulets, tips and taps of snow wads
heavied, chunking down from pine boughs,
a raven bathing in a moss-filled tub.
In her grave, the cat's body brews
a fester round her bones. The stones
atop it mark it as a grave. The raven,
incapable of sadness, flutters a silver froth
into the air around it. So the man goes walking.

Time was, nothing was, which is to say
the world might be imagined, might have been

a sin everything is responsible for.
When he reaches the elephant rock, an elephant
buried the rain has half-exhumed, he sits
on the brow of what had been a great intelligence
of stone, and imagines an elephant's sadness.
The sky is a single cloud, elephant colored.
There's a snail drowned in a depression.

More reasonable than oceans are lakes, ponds
more reasonable still, tarns in their stillness
sublime with calm. And most of all
these puddles beyond counting, one
between his boots, in which a snail is reborn,
climbing over most of an hour a single inch
onto a twig, where it raises its delicate horns
and basks like a saint. Asking only that it be so,
the man is the mother of an elephant's dream.

4. Lonely Soul
". . . the inconceivable idea of the sun." —Stevens

The whole body's phantom in the afterlife,
an indelible ache to feel felt only
as the absence of feeling. To see and taste
nothing but the memory of what had been,
to smell nothing but the scent of nothing.
Though it may be so only for the soul,
the body feeling its way into the body
of the earth, a gigantic sexual union
the soul, being bodiless, cannot apprehend.

At last the body, freed from the need
to understand, understands its need
in its own terms, while the soul imagines the nothing
of being, of being nothing more than a soul.

And yet, as the body becomes nothing,
the soul hangs on in its body's past, its fleshbook,
its pains and satisfactions, imagining,
as the body cannot, the slink of the flesh
into the afterlife, the afterlife its only witness.

And yet the soul sees nothing, no taste
of the sweetness of death, no bloat, no gnaw
as the plinth of its body disintegrates—as the column
it was, from the capital vault to the spinal shaft,
evaporates—and it wonders, the soul,
at the inconceivable idea of the hand.
Fine pentacular gatherer, bringer into the light
and the darkness all that once was held
for the delectation partly of the brain, the soul spark

and seed of this imagined phantomness.
Prickle of the skin, gooseflesh, thirst,
and tumescence, and the awareness even then
it did not feel but categorized feeling,
a taxonomer of sensation, processor of pleasure
and agony, the lonely soul vaporous
among vapors that once had had bodies too.
Imagine the ellipse of salt the fingertip was, licked
ten thousand times to turn a page.

5. Body
"Except when he escapes from it." —*Stevens*

The age of the final nostalgia, proverbs
of the pines, a mother tree the man,
having considered the risks, climbs
nevertheless, pocketing bird nests abandoned,
engaging in a momentary preachment

to an owl clenched upon a branch
draped with eviscerated hides and bones.
Who sees the tree's reality? No one
but an owl the man believes might be someone.

Near the top, the pine's main spar, clutched
between and more slender than his thighs,
sways in windlessness from his weight.
He waits and sways, then climbs two
and three more limb rungs and reaches
slowly up to stroke once the green
shivering ghost that is the topmost whisk.
He is lover of heaven and lover of earth,
in a kind of paradise, destitute and glad.

More difficult by a factor of nine
the descent, repassing the disconcerted owl
that still does not fly. By the time he reaches
earth again his gloves are gloved with pitch
and scales, bark shards and cone grit,
an itch in his shirt where two last nests are tucked.
It may be that climbing a tree is a body's
way of understanding, climbing down
the surrender to the soul's uncertainty again.

There was almost a moment when he almost
understood his body understood the world
his imagination had laid out before him,
when what was imagined was what the body knew
and of which the imagination made its use.
It was a world there was no knowledge of
in the world, and the world was a system
he was lost in, synagogue and cathedral,
chapel in which everything that was was true.

In the homophone of its hoo, the owl pronounced
what he was, a thing alive in love with the world.
Now the wind rose and the meadow grasses
swirled and the owl soared into the distance
and vanished, in love with air, acknowledging earth.
Living where and as he lived, the man walked,
moving as a man over the body of the world
as over the body of the beloved,
something else he might never understand.

The greatest poverty was to live on the earth
believing it could not be understood,
the body being one with it and the brain
believing it mattered what the brain believed:
that the earth was a place and not a destiny,
an October of the spirit, destined to be doomed
but invigorated at the top of a tree,
where its body had taken it, willingly,
that it might feel and taste, hear and smell, and see.

THE NEW MOUSETRAP

Whether it is better, I cannot say:
a hammer, a platform, a catch, a spring,
the spring, the summer, the winter, the fall,
they all, every season, for the reason
of food and shelter, somehow come inside,
despite the cat, despite the batts of steel wool
in every oubliette and fissure jammed—

but just now, no more than five steps away
from the pantry door, I hear the new trap slam
and return to find not one mouse, but two—
cute, almost adorable gray vermin
instantly killed there. So perhaps
the long goad of industry has attained
that acme long sought, the epitome

of me or you or us against them—
harborers of hantavirus, leavers
to us of the commas of their black curds,
as these vanquished two after death still do,
though they quiver not, nor in the least way
give they any other sign of life,
which will end, if more slowly, for us all.

A FEW ITEMS AT THIS MOMENT

The sky is cloudless and there is no wind.
Wholly encased in snow, the trees
at the mountaintop are not beyond
words but beyond my willingness

to diminish them, their blue shadows,
the silence. There are a few items
at this moment no one in the world knows
but me, and I choose not to say them,

not even to the mountain or the trees,
to whom they would not matter anyway,
being in all ways wordless,
having absolutely nothing to say

about a man who's merely come this way
and does not speak and cannot stay.

PROUST

By the light of my reading lamp, she regards me,
or studies the shape of me where I sit,
the shadow I am, she being mostly blind.
She's lying on the couch, and it may be
she is uncertain I am even here, for she was asleep
when I entered the room and took my place
to read. And before I picked up
my book, it was I who studied her,
so slight and barely visible was her breathing.
Only the dream twitch of a paw made me know
she was alive. So I began. Then somewhere
in the midst of *Swann's Way*, I became aware
of her again. I felt her looking at me
and lowered my book, and peered over
my glasses to see her, her pupils large
and besilvered milkily. And now we have been
looking at one another for a long time,
I waiting for her to lay her head down and sleep again,
she wondering if the dark stillness,
available to her as scent at least, is me
or the ghost of me in my chair, there
even when I am not. And since I am wondering
what next endless memory will be taken up,
and wondering also how long our mutual study
might last, I rise and watch over my shoulder
as she traces the shadow of my going
to the pantry, where I fetch her
one of the biscuits she loves.

BOX

The little barn, built entirely of cherrywood—studs, beams,
      rafters, braces, even the battened siding,
from the trees of the vanished orchard before it—was unusual
      in that pineless, hardwood-only land, and by then,
in the time my father and his friend disassembled it,
      worth a fortune—theirs, if only they would take it away.

And that's what they did, four flatbed truckloads they divided
      in equal portions, each to his own woodshop.
From those stacks over the years emerged desks,
      chairs, tables, and shelves, cabinets and chifforobes,
picture frames and coatracks and an elaborately dovetailed
      carryall box my father made, and in which, for years now,

I have saved postcards from friends all over the world.
      A year after my father's death, there's still a substantial pile
of cherrywood awaiting plane, saw, and chisel, awaiting his hands
      or the hands of his friend, who is also dead, so that now
this pile is mine, along with many tools I do not know how
      to use, though I intend to learn to, a little, at least.

I would like to make something of cherrywood, something
      a man with a completely other kind of patience
and skill might make, someone who has devoted his life
      to the joinery of words, to the containment of meaning
and implication, little boxes the practicality of which,
      let alone the purpose, might seem, at best, elusive.

A bookcase, I'm thinking. Square and upright sides,
      with routed kerfs into which its shelves might be fitted,
a built-up base shoed in a simple molding,
      a matching bonnet, similarly molded and mitered.

Here and there in the stock, small square nail holes
	my father would have filled invisibly, but which I will leave,

in honor of the barn he and his friend spent a week
	disassembling fifty years ago, leaving also these two
or three dimples from a crowbar, which they would have
	planed away, having minds inclined toward perfection,
something a man in my line of work does not quite believe in—
	a feeling I do not think my father would have understood.

After all, the carryall box where the postcards are is perfect.
	And I love the postcards too, most of them
saying only the usual things that are said on such cards.
	When he gave me the box, I asked my father
what's this for? And he responded, "Anything that will fit.
	Anything you can imagine."

CONSERVATOR'S STATEMENT

Things, stuff, keepsakes, doodads;
junk, curios, and conversation pieces; souvenirs,
trinkets, paraphernalia, and oddball collectibles.
Items ineffably indisposable, whatnots
and weird effects, worthless and invaluable.
Memorabilia, mementos, weird magnets
and rigmarole, matchbooks and bones,
shed antlers, the hoof of an elk hollowed out
by years of a river's flow: fundamentally useless
freight to be foisted upon one's heirs someday.
Little box made of birchwood, someone's
lost fob of keys inside. Ticket stubs and a stob
of tree limb in the shape of a broken heart.
A bowl of *Letharia vulpina*, wolf lichen,
growing ever more luminous as it dries.
The collarbone of a hare, for literary reasons.
Seasonal wrack, elephantine maple leaf forgotten and flattened
in a book of photographs of old-time loggers.
Clutch of nine whistles whistled once.
Conundra, paradoxical pieces of other pieces
of sanctified crap, mostly figurative,
except for a pair of owl pellets sealed in spray lacquer
lest they disintegrate; from one, the skull
of a mouse peering into the air of the room.
Also an actual coprolite, fossilized literal shit.
Unbeloved treasure, doubloons of detritus,
memorial markers, evidence of passage
and testimonials of a seeing one would wish
to be deeper, imaginative chits and vouchers,
assurances that one was, that one had been,
that one had walked through the world
perceiving heaven. The Champion spark plug

ensheathed in amalgamated stone and sand,
little engine of remembering, bric-a-brac
gimcrackery, doohickey amulets, froufrou
found and undocumented, haphazardly curated
and placed in places where each might be,
for the finder or a passerby, acknowledged
in bewilderment or amazement or a rush of recall,
as what was, and so acknowledged, still is.

About the only thing I thought I knew
was that nothing I'd ever know would do
any good. Sunrise, say, or that the part
of the horse's hoof that most resembles
a human palm is called the frog;
certain chords on the guitar of no mercantile use;
the abstruse circuitry of an envelope
quatrain; even the meaning of horripilation.

Sometimes on a flatland mound the ancients had made,
I took heart in the pointlessness of stars
and lay there until my teeth chattered.
I earned my last Boy Scout merit badge
building a birdhouse out of license plates
manufactured by felons in the big house.
No more paramilitary organizations for me,
I said, ten years before I was drafted.

I had skills. Sure-footedness and slick
fielding. Eventually I would learn to unhook
a bra one-handed, practicing on my friend,
his sister's worn over his T-shirt (I took
my turns too). One Easter Sunday I hid
through the church service among the pipes
of the organ and still did not have faith,
although my ears rang until Monday.

I began to know that little worth knowing
was knowable and faith was delusion.
I began to believe I believed in believing
nothing I was supposed to believe in,
except the stars, which, like me,

were not significant, except for their light,
meaning I loved them for their pointlessness.
I believed I owned them somehow.

A C major 7th chord was beautiful and almost rare.
The horse I loved foundered and had to be
put down. The middle rhyme in an envelope
quatrain was not imprisoned if it was right.
In cold air a nipple horripilates
and rises, the sun comes up and up and up,
a star that bakes the eggs
in a Boy Scout license plate birdhouse.

God was in music and music was God.
A drill sergeant seized me by my dog tag
chain and threatened to beat me
to a pile of bloody guts for the peace sign
I'd chiseled in the first of my two tags,
the one he said they'd leave in my mouth
before they zipped the body bag closed.
Yet one more thing I'd come to know.

He also said that Uncle Sam owned my ass,
no more true than my ownership
of the stars. I can play a C major 7th chord
in five or six places on the neck of a guitar.
A stabled horse's frog degrades; a wild horse's
becomes a callus, smooth as leather.
Stars are invisible in rainy weather,
something any fool knows, of course.

ANCIENT RAIN

Here comes the rain, the same rain
in the round of its long cycle
that might have fallen
on Horace or Szymborska, on Rilke

or Stalin, even on the bushes
long since become the soil
today's rain enriches,
bringing forth this week the small

five-petaled yellow glacier lilies,
first wildflowers of the year.
Before scarlet gilia,
before lupine, even before shooting stars,

all of which have risen
for centuries over this mountainside,
where I have lived only a couple dozen
of the years I have been allotted,

which have seemed more or less the same
to the trees and the lilies,
as the rain seems also the same,
falling, just now, on me.

GALLOP

The yellow pines thrash their manes
        and rear. You can almost hear
beneath their stationary hooves
        the billion root-hairs clench and click,
their nickers and neighs. A nowhere wind
        goes by on the way to nowhere else,
bringing joy and panic to the trees.
        In the interludes between gusts
they shuffle and sway then stand
        almost immobile in the downpour
of shed needles—finally only a single branch
        bobbing like a twitched flank.
Then stillness, the sound of what was
        fading in the east, the sound of what's coming
coming nearer from the west. They grow
        restive. They wait until the wind comes
and gallop in their stillness again.

ELK

His hindquarters fell through the ice,
and he could not pull himself out,
and the incoming colder weather
refroze the hole around him and he died,
only the forelegs and broad horns
holding his head and neck above the surface.

Soon he was discovered by coyotes,
who ate all they could. His face, that is,
the soft just-frozen cheeks and muzzle,
the tongue, which would have protruded
from his open dying mouth; then
the tearing of the throat, the coyotes'
prints visible only in the sheen of blood
around the snowless black surface of the lake.

Such cold this soon in winter, autumn really,
still early December, has surprised us all,
and since snow is in the forecast this afternoon,
I have come to skate. I'm half a mile from shore
when I see him, or see what's left,
and reconstruct the story of his demise.

The coyotes ignored his spraddled legs,
hoof points still borne down against the pull
of his back half. A six-point bull elk,
some abrasions on the surface of the ice
where the horns thrashed but held him up.

A half-mile skate back to where I hung my boots
from a limb, a hundred-yard walk from there
to the truck, where I keep a bow saw

I could use to remove a wedge of pate
with the perfect rack of horns, but I choose not to.
Something in the weariness of the bones
of his jaw, also the snow just now beginning.

Given the altitude here, he'll be completely covered
in a month, and at breakup, late March
or early April, he will sink as he did not yesterday
or the day before or the day before that, and the bones
and horns of him will settle to the bottom.

Still, the coyotes may be back tonight,
to nose their ways behind the horns' main shafts
to the ears, which I notice are still upright and whole,
the left one turned slightly farther left,
as though, with the last of his miraculous senses,
he'd heard them coming over the ice.

BEING A LAKE

He has never dreamed of being a lake
in the high mountains, and now he wonders why.
Surely there could be no better, in the way
of dreamy aspirations: to be clear and cold
and swum through by trout. To allow the sunlight
far into your depths, to have depths no one
will ever visit. To be ceilinged by ice
and many feet of snow in winter, to shine pure blue
into the pure blue of the sky, to show the stars
the stars, to be drunk by wild animals.
And to admit an occasional human,
who, because of the memory of having been there,
might dream of being there. Being there.
Not a visitor but a dreamer, dreaming
this very lake is what he's always wanted to be.

HERE

Not that it must be seen, nor that its sounds—
a squawking quail, a constant easy wind
strumming limbs and needles—must be made clear.
The winter-killed doe's inconsequential;
that smell of spring earth, though monumental,
has no significance whatsoever

to anything not now nourished by it.
No, the new season has never once thought
itself a figure, a trope, a symbol.
Signified, but knowing no signifier.
Still, the black expanse from last year's slash fire
offers a tiny, succulent morel.

That I leave it there is mere self-interest.
Let it seed the entire forest
with its kind, so I might have more someday.
I would share them then, but you are not here
and will not be when I array them there
on a dark blue platter, freshly sautéed.

I'm sorry. This is not about your life
but mine. I don't know who you are, or if,
in fact, you are there at all, though hope, I do,
that you might still be able to savor
some of the sublime, buttered earth flavor
of what, if only in this way, I offer you.

NOTES

The Francis Ponge epigraph is taken from "The Crate," in *The Voice of Things*, translated by Beth Archer (New York: McGraw-Hill, 1972).

The epigraph from Wallace Stevens is taken from "Parochial Theme," in *The Collected Poems of Wallace Stevens* (New York: Alfred A. Knopf, 1954).

Though it is about me and my father, "A Fine Boy" is dedicated to the memory of C. K. Williams.

"Brother to Jackdaws": Linnaeus classified the bird as *Corvus monedula*. *Monedula* derives from *moneta*, the Latin stem of the word *money*. It is said that Eurasian jackdaws are very fond of coins.

"Mother Country": In addition to the five epigraphs, which are taken from "Esthétique du Mal" and "Notes Toward a Supreme Fiction," there are several phrases in the sequence adapted from the poems of Wallace Stevens.

ACKNOWLEDGMENTS

Thanks to the editors of the following publications, in which (sometimes in somewhat revised forms) these poems first appeared:

The American Journal of Poetry: Human Knowledge

Antiphon (UK): Raven in April

Cascadia Review: Box

Clackamas Literary Review: A Few Items at This Moment

Conduit: Elk

Ecotone: The New Mousetrap

Fogged Clarity: His Previous Life as a Lichen; Proust

The Georgia Review: Stillness, Waiting

Hampden-Sydney Poetry Review: Here; Tinnitus

Iron Horse Literary Review: Ancient Rain

The Kenyon Review: Conservator's Statement

The Literary Review: Ecology

Little Star: Mother Country

The Moth (Ireland): Sheep in Umbria

Numéro Cinq: Or Possibly Languor

Permafrost: Because the Mountain Dwarfs the Grove, the Sky the Mountain (under the title "Aspen Grove")

Poetry Salzburg Review (Austria): S. Francesco; Visit Beautiful Assisi

Shenandoah: Being a Lake

The Southampton Review: Jasmine (under the title "Bougain-villea"); Mio Dio

Southern Indiana Review: Blessed Are

Terrain: Gallop

TLS (*Times Literary Supplement*, UK): Thee

"Blessed Are" also appeared in *The Best American Poetry 2014*, selected by Terrance Hayes, edited by David Lehman (New York: Scribner, 2014).

"Ecology" also appeared in *Dark Mountain Poetics*, Vol. 10 (Southwold, UK: Dark Mountain, 2016).

"Elk" also appeared in *Pushcart Prize XLI: Best of the Small Presses*, edited by Bill Henderson (Wainscott, NY: Pushcart Press, 2017).

"From the Perspective of the Meadow" first appeared in *The Echoing Green: Poems of Fields, Meadows, and Grasses*, edited by Cecily Parks (New York: Penguin Random House, 2016).

Robert Wrigley is the author of ten collections of poetry, including, most recently, *Anatomy of Melancholy and Other Poems* (Penguin, 2013), which won a 2014 Pacific Northwest Book Award. His earlier books have been awarded the Kingsley Tufts Award, the San Francisco Poetry Center Book Award, and the Poets' Prize. A University Distinguished Professor Emeritus at the University of Idaho, he lives in the woods near Moscow, Idaho, with his wife, the writer Kim Barnes.

PENGUIN POETS

JOHN ASHBERY
Selected Poems
Self-Portrait in a Convex Mirror

PAUL BEATTY
Joker, Joker, Deuce

JOSHUA BENNETT
The Sobbing School

TED BERRIGAN
The Sonnets

LAUREN BERRY
The Lifting Dress

PHILIP BOOTH
Lifelines: Selected Poems 1950–1999

JULIANNE BUCHSBAUM
The Apothecary's Heir

JIM CARROLL
Fear of Dreaming: The Selected Poems
Living at the Movies
Void of Course

ALISON HAWTHORNE DEMING
Genius Loci
Rope
Stairway to Heaven

CARL DENNIS
Another Reason
Callings
New and Selected Poems 1974–2004
Practical Gods
Ranking the Wishes
Unknown Friends

DIANE DI PRIMA
Loba

STUART DISCHELL
Dig Safe

STEPHEN DOBYNS
Velocities: New and Selected Poems: 1966–1992

EDWARD DORN
Way More West

ROGER FANNING
The Middle Ages

ADAM FOULDS
The Broken Word

CARRIE FOUNTAIN
Burn Lake
Instant Winner

AMY GERSTLER
Crown of Weeds
Dearest Creature
Ghost Girl
Medicine
Nerve Storm
Scattered at Sea

EUGENE GLORIA
Drivers at the Short-Time Motel
Hoodlum Birds
My Favorite Warlord

DEBORA GREGER
By Herself
Desert Fathers, Uranium Daughters
God
Men, Women, and Ghosts
Western Art

TERRANCE HAYES
Hip Logic
How to Be Drawn
Lighthead
Wind in a Box

NATHAN HOKS
The Narrow Circle

ROBERT HUNTER
Sentinel and Other Poems

MARY KARR
Viper Rum

JACK KEROUAC
Book of Blues
Book of Haikus
Book of Sketches

JOANNA KLINK
Circadian
Excerpts from a Secret Prophecy
Raptus

JOANNE KYGER
As Ever: Selected Poems

ANN LAUTERBACH
Hum
If in Time: Selected Poems, 1975–2000
On a Stair
Or to Begin Again
Under the Sign

CORINNE LEE
Plenty

PHILLIS LEVIN
May Day
Mercury
Mr. Memory & Other Poems

PATRICIA LOCKWOOD
Motherland Fatherland Homelandsexuals

WILLIAM LOGAN
Macbeth in Venice
Madame X
Strange Flesh
The Whispering Gallery

ADRIAN MATEJKA
The Big Smoke
Map to the Stars
Mixology

MICHAEL MCCLURE
Huge Dreams: San Francisco and Beat Poems

ROSE MCLARNEY
Its Day Being Gone

DAVID MELTZER
David's Copy: The Selected Poems of David Meltzer

ROBERT MORGAN
Dark Energy
Terroir

CAROL MUSKE-DUKES
An Octave above Thunder
Red Trousseau
Twin Cities

ALICE NOTLEY
Certain Magical Acts
Culture of One
The Descent of Alette
Disobedience
In the Pines
Mysteries of Small Houses

WILLIE PERDOMO
The Essential Hits of Shorty Bon Bon

LIA PURPURA
It Shouldn't Have Been Beautiful

LAWRENCE RAAB
The History of Forgetting
Visible Signs: New and Selected Poems

BARBARA RAS
The Last Skin
One Hidden Stuff

MICHAEL ROBBINS
Alien vs. Predator
The Second Sex

PATTIANN ROGERS
Generations
Holy Heathen Rhapsody
Wayfare

ROBYN SCHIFF
A Woman of Property

WILLIAM STOBB
Absentia
Nervous Systems

TRYFON TOLIDES
An Almost Pure Empty Walking

SARAH VAP
Viability

ANNE WALDMAN
Gossamurmur
Kill or Cure
Manatee/Humanity
Structure of the World Compared to a Bubble

JAMES WELCH
Riding the Earthboy 40

PHILIP WHALEN
Overtime: Selected Poems

ROBERT WRIGLEY
Anatomy of Melancholy and Other Poems
Beautiful Country
Box
Earthly Meditations: New and Selected Poems
Lives of the Animals
Reign of Snakes

MARK YAKICH
The Importance of Peeling Potatoes in Ukraine
Unrelated Individuals Forming a Group Waiting to Cross